My Life Interrupted, Not Once, but Forever

A Play

By Trena Bolden Fields

Bolden Fields Media

2015

Published in St. Louis Park, Minnesota, by Trena Bolden Fields/Bolden Fields Media, 5775 Wayzata Boulevard Suite 700, St. Louis Park, MN 55416. This play may be purchased in bulk for educational or fundraising purposes. For more information, please email trena@trenaboldenfields.com.

DEDICATION

This play is dedicated to all individuals navigating a life
interrupted.

AKNOWLEDGEMENTS

I would like to say thank you to my family, especially my husband, Jerome, and daughters, Kayla and Annaleece. Thank you for allowing me to share my journey with the world. Thank you to Sarah Myers and the faculty of Augsburg College's MFA Creative Writing Program for your unwavering support of my work. Thank you Raye Birk and The Actors Workout for the space and encouragement you have provided throughout the years. Thank you Jamil Jude for your direction, for helping me organize this piece and gain clarity. Thank you Mom, Jerome, Ayesha Adu, James A. Moad, II and Douglas Scott Allen for your editing assistance. Thank you to Sonja, Jacqueline, Lloyd, Beth and Phyllis too…for without all of you this work would've been much harder to write.

SUMMARY

My Life Interrupted, Not Once, but Forever

Trena Bolden Fields

My Life Interrupted, Not Once, but Forever is a coming of age play about one woman's journey navigating through marriage, motherhood and living abroad as the wife of a diplomat. In the play we see the main character move from being a fulfilled actor to working to reshape her identity after many life interruptions.

My Life Interrupted, Not Once, but Forever premiered in the Minnesota Fringe Festival at the New Century Theatre on August 2, 2015. This play was originally produced as a one-woman show and performed by Trena Bolden Fields. Jamil Jude was the director with sound design by Derek "Duck" Washington, stage managed by Beth Desotelle and prop and costume design by Phyllis Hankerson.

CAST

Trena/Jerome/Papa/Mamma/Wise
Persons/Kayla/Annaleece…………..Trena Bolden Fields
Neighbor………………………...voice of Beth Desotelle
Guard……………………………...voice of Foster Johns
Jerome……………………………voice of Jerome Fields
Kayla………………………………voice of Kayla Fields
Annaleece………………………voice of Annaleece Fields

CHARACTERS

Trena, a giving actress who wants to do more with her career

Kayla, an extremely energetic determined youngster who is a dreamer

Annaleece, a bashful determined and organized child who loves fashion

Jerome, an intelligent down to earth diplomat with large aspirations

Sister/Wise Person 1
Mom/Wise Person 2
Papa/Wise Person 3/Guard
Supervisor/Neighbor/Wise Person 4

SETTING

Multiple locations, mainly Trena's homes throughout her life and travels: her college dorm room, parents' home, aunt and uncle's home, house in Minnesota, an apartment in D.C., house in Mexico, house in D.C., apartment in Minnesota, and house in Pretoria, South Africa. Settings can be adapted based on stage size and availability.

PRELUDE

(Present day. Lights up. TRENA is sitting, holding a book. The intercom buzzes. She puts down the book.)

TRENA

Hello.

GUARD
(South African accent)
Good morning, Ma'am! How are you this morning?

TRENA

Fine—thank you! How are you?

GUARD

Fine. Thank you. Rohan is here to fix your garage.

TRENA

Okay. Thank you. You can let him in.

NEIGHBOR

Hey Trena! We are heading out of town for the weekend. Jerome said you all will watch the cats.

TRENA

Oh, yeah.

NEIGHBOR

Here is the key so you can check on our cats.

TRENA

Sure thing!

ANNALEECE

Mommy, Mommy, Mommy!

CAT

Meow!

ANNALEECE

Mommy, Mommy, Mommy! My teacher says I can bring a swimsuit to school tomorrow!

TRENA

Oh, yeah! How exciting!

ANNALEECE

Yeah!

KAYLA

Mom, can I bake a cake?

DOG

Woof, Woof, Woof!

(*The cat and the new dog are running around. The cat is hissing at the dog.*)

TRENA
(*To KAYLA*)

Honey! No, mommy is getting ready to fix breakfast. Did you wash your face and brush your teeth?

KAYLA

Oh! I forgot. (*Chuckles*)

TRENA

You, too, Anna.

ANNALEECE

But that's boring! Brushing your teeth is boring!

TRENA

NOW!

(*Kids run upstairs. TRENA peeks outside and then starts breakfast.*)

JEROME

Hon, can you iron my shirt for me please?

TRENA

Kids…and cats…and dogs…and husbands…they can suck the life out of you, can't they? (*Pause*) Now my head hurts. (*Talking to the animals*) Move out of my way so I can get to what I can get to. They walking around here like I owe them something. Like I don't have nothing to do. I got needs of my own. Let's see.

(*Pulls out a planner full of committed times. Picking up the book.*)

TRENA (*cont.*)

I wish I had more time to read. I think I can catch a half hour while I'm waiting for the girls to finish gymnastics, but no (*Putting down the book*)...I can catch an hour right before bedtime. I'll try that.

(*Kids tapping at her stomach at the same time to get her attention.*)

ANNALEECE

Mommy, Mommy, Mommy!

TRENA

Yes.

ANNALEECE

I am a big ghurl aren't I?

TRENA

Yes, you are, honey.

KAYLA

Mom, Mom, Mom!

TRENA

Yes, cupcake.

KAYLA

I am not a cupcake. I am a flower.

TRENA

Oh, okay.

KAYLA

Mom, Mom, Mom! I made a story about a cat who likes to jump really high and the crow who ran down the road.

TRENA

Oh, really?

KAYLA

Yes, and it stars a girl who loves animals and trees and plants and science and dance and soccer and gymnastics and she wants to be everyfing when she grows up!

TRENA

Really! (*To audience*) Who needs a book when they have colorful stories like these to listen to? This is a typical day at my house, yet how did I get here?

(*Lights shift*)

SCENE 1

(It is 1997. *18-year-old TRENA is praying.*)

TRENA
Well, Lord, what I would like to do is become a professional model and actor doing movies and singing gospel music. I want to do all of these things to glorify you. I don't want anyone or anything to step in my way or my path…meaning, I don't want anything to hinder me. I want you, Father God, to continually direct my path as I continually acknowledge you and pray to you, Father God. Amen. (*To audience*) In college I prayed constantly and for my ideal life. Not only did I pray for it, but I worked hard to build my acting chops; auditioning for plays, taking classes and training to make something of myself. As an actor, I could do both August Wilson and Shakespeare.

(*TRENA performs two one-minute monologues: Berniece from The Piano Lesson by August Wilson[1] and Emilia from Othello by William Shakespeare[2].*)

TRENA (*cont.*)
Pretty good for an 18-year old. I had some skills, huh! Being *this* into acting, what in the world could come between me and my dream?

(*Lights shift*)

---

[1] Wilson, August, *The Piano Lesson* (Plume: 1990).
[2] Shakespeare, William, *Othello* (The Plays of Shakespeare, Volume III. Reprinted by Gramercy Books: 1979).

SCENE 2

TRENA

In 1997, I was so focused on my career that I did not have time for anything else…not even a relationship. Thinking about having my heart broken from my parents' separation and divorce was one reason why I told my family that I would not be dating anytime soon and never having kids. I was working on decreasing my potentialities to have family drama. I remember how my life was interrupted when I was three years old.

(*Remembering parents' separation*)

MOM

Girls, we will have to move in with your aunt and uncle until Mommy can get on her feet.

TRENA
(*To audience*)
My mom said as we walked towards my aunt and uncle's house after the dramatic parting of ways with my father—and, yes, there was a hammer and a chair involved. No. No one got hurt, just harsh words and serious threats. Moving in with my aunt and uncle had its own challenges, and it began with me…eh um, being "melodramatic." The very next morning, (*TRENA is three years old crying like a baby.*) Wah, wah, wah. (*To audience*) My aunt called me out.

AUNT

There she go again acting like a baby and being melodramatic.

TRENA

I wasn't being melodramatic, I was three years old! Did anybody realize that I really did not understand how to process my interrupted life?…nope. We just went on. In my own dating life, I dealt with relationship drama after relationship drama—situations like, "Trena, I love you," and then I would find out all the other women that were being loved by the same man or I dealt with guys who I only wanted to be friends with wanting to be more than friends with me, like this kid I met in college. It was the fall of 1997, he walked into a house on Augsburg College's campus that housed an office that supported students from African descent. We both had a scholarship from the Pan-Afrikan program. We met. He said, "Hi!" I said, "Hi." We kept in

TRENA (*cont.*)

touch. That summer he helped me move back to my parents' house in Crystal, Minnesota.

MOM

Trena, who is that?

TRENA

Oh, just a friend from college.

PAPA

Hey son, what did you say your name is?

JEROME

Jerome.

PAPA

Oh, nice to meet you.

MOM

Why not date him?

TRENA

Stop it! He is just my friend from college. Papa and Mom, stop looking at him like that.

MOM

I'm just saying; you might want to think about him instead of the bozos you date.

TRENA
(*To audience*)

She would say something like that. (*To family*) Look, no more dating advice. We need to have a meeting. (*To audience*) I called my sister and invited her over and later that evening, I said…

(*TRENA and family are sitting in the living room on the couch.*)

TRENA (*cont.*)

Sister, Mom, Papa, I need to tell you something. (*To audience*) Papa is my step-father who has been in my life since I was 11. (*To MOM, PAPA, and SISTER*) I'm not interested in dating anyone or settling down and I am not planning on having any kids. So this means Mom

TRENA (*cont.*)

and Papa, will not be able to be grandparents to my kids and, Sister, you won't be able to be a fabulous aunt like I am to your kids. Is this okay with you?

MOM

It's your body.

PAPA

Yeah, you have to be okay with that.

SISTER

It's your life.

TRENA

"Thank God!" I thought. This time, I wasn't accused of being "melodramatic" and they actually responded favorably. Two years went by and Jerome and I remained friends, until one day, he tried the unthinkable. It was after a night out together just doing friend stuff. We had just returned to my dorm.

JEROME

Trena, um, uh, um. Uh. I, um, uh.

TRENA

Jerome, what are you trying to say?

JEROME

Um, uh, um.

TRENA

Jerome, spit it out.

JEROME

I, uh, um.

TRENA

If you don't spit it out, I am going to go to bed. (*To audience*) It was late and I didn't really know how to tell him that all I wanted was his friendship. His stammering was my way out. And that was the last I saw of him for a while. He did not talk to me for the next four years.

(*Sound of a door slam. Lights shift.*)

SCENE 3

TRENA
It was 2003, no husband, no kids, and I was on the path to achieving my dream; acting on stages and in film. Yes, I was planning to do it BIG and wanted to do it BIGGER. On and on I auditioned, booking roles at Twin Cities' theatres and in film. (*Remembering*) Coming out of college, producers and directors were impressed with my resume. I had a history of professional work. I booked a touring contract and was working full-time as an actor! I was beginning to live my dream! But, I realized, my student loans were due. I know you know how that goes. My reality was interrupted with the reality that I could be a starving artist. My first "coming off tour being a *real* adult" full time job was great. I had a regular salary. I worked with fun and fabulous people, but this creative soul was deflated by the need to make sales calls daily. Most of the day, my head was on my desk. Sorry boss. While living in my new reality, I got the call of my next interruption.

(Phone rings)

SUPERVISOR
Trena, we are in need of an interim director for the Pan-Afrikan Center and your potential predecessor said that if we should call anyone, it should be you. Are you available?

TRENA
(To audience)
I made an impression on the previous program director while in college! Thank God! (*Into the phone*) YES! How much is the pay? (*To audience*) It was a few thousand more than what I was making. I made the switch the very next month. What? This was my way of settling into my life interrupted. Really, I was too chicken to be the artist I was born to be. BUT, I worked that job like nobody's business. I used my creative juices to help others. I even decided to get my Master's in Educational Psychology from the University of Minnesota, yeah, I know–but what about acting?…I thought I'd always do that, but in the moment what I needed to do was figure out how I was going to do this new interruption…Once I figured it out, I began acting again…picking up shows at well-known theatres. First, understudying for a play at the History Theatre and then for a production of *Joe Turner's Come and*

TRENA (*cont.*)
Gone at Penumbra. The most exciting experience at the time was playing Ruby in Penumbra's production of August Wilson's *Seven Guitars*...

(*TRENA performs a short monologue as Ruby from <u>Seven Guitars</u>[3].*)

TRENA (*cont.*)
I also performed in commercials and did print work...I was working my nine to five, going to rehearsal from six to 11 and hoping for my big break...

(*Lights shift*)

---

[3] Wilson, August, *Seven Guitars* (Plume: 1997).

SCENE 4

TRENA

But, I started to long for a relationship…for a deep loving relationship. As a 24-year-old, I was really looking for true love and respect. What? I didn't want to experience my life nor my big break alone…a girl needs love. I remembered the time when a very nerdy, but respectful friend helped me move home from college and how that friend may have been interested in me some time ago. So I emailed him. (*Typing*) Dear Jerome, I hope you are well! I am writing to just say "hi". Are you still in London? (*To audience*) He responded right away.

JEROME

Hi Trena! How are you? Actually I will be moving back to Minnesota in a few weeks. I'll get in touch when I am back in town.

TRENA

Oh my goodness! He called me a few weeks after being in town and asked me to meet him at the *Great Minnesota Get-Together*. So I dragged my sister and nephews along with me. And the third thing that came out of Jerome's mouth was…

JEROME

So are you seeing someone?

TRENA
(*To audience*)
Oh my! Okay, be cool. (*To JEROME*) No, are you?

JEROME

No. I would like to hang out sometime.

TRENA
(*To self*)
He forgave me! Thank God! (*To JEROME*) Okay. Let's do that. (*To audience*) So we went out for a "date." I didn't really realize it was an official "date" until I saw how nice the restaurant was. Honestly, I was still feeling him out…seeing if we were going to be good friends or if he was into me… I caught on mid-way through the "date." Then we started hanging out almost every other day. Who would've thought within our first three weeks of really hanging out with each other, he would say….

JEROME

I want us to date <u>exclusively</u>!

(*Sound of a record scratch*)

TRENA

I mean, okay, a little hard on the gas pedal. A little hard on the gas pedal. My response was…

(*Sound of chirping crickets*)

TRENA (*cont.*)

"Okay." Two weeks later we were hanging out at my apartment. Nothing serious. He looked like he had something on his mind, so I said, "Jerome, what is going on?"

JEROME

Oh, nothing.

TRENA

Tell me. What is it?

JEROME
(*Pause*)

I, I, I don't know if I am ready…

TRENA

Ready for?

JEROME

To say what's on my mind.

TRENA

Just go ahead and tell me. (*To audience*) I'm thinking, we've been friends like forever…he should be able to talk to me, right?

JEROME

I love you!

(*Chirping crickets*)

TRENA

Okay…Really hard on the gas pedal. Three months later, he proposed. I said yes, and eight months later we tied the knot. Did we move too fast? Was I really ready for marriage? All I know is my attention turned to loving him and creating a life together. Within weeks after our marriage, the questions began...

JEROME

So when are we going to work on our family?

(*Loud chirping crickets!*)

TRENA

In five years. *(To audience)* Being a busy program director and still budding actress while working on my master's, I was, again, not planning to have children. Who had time for babies? A year went by…

JEROME

Sooo when are we going to work on our family?

TRENA

In five years.

JEROME

You said that last year!

TRENA

I know. (*To audience*) The BIG question was…Was I ready for kids? Remember my conversation with my parents and sister? Remember my budding acting career? Boy, I do. So after another few months, I decided that I would pray about having kids: "God, I want you to know that I am open to this. I am open to having kids if this is the life for me. If it is for me to have kids, please change my heart and mind." (*To audience*) Didn't I want to, to procreate, and help make this world a better place by producing well-adjusted kids? I began to want it. I began to trust love and the beauty of creation… And after two babies in the first four years of our marriage, including midnight feedings, diaper changes and tag teaming staying up all night rocking tired babies— (*Aside*) Did I say I was ready? Really?—I now realize I was barely ready to figure out my own life, let alone two others…the things we do for money and love.

(*Lights shift*)

SCENE 5

TRENA

It was 2008 and working for others started to drive me crazy. With
eight-month-old, Kayla, at home, I was also experiencing stress on a
new job. I decided to quit working for others, stay home with my
daughter and find other ways to create income. "Um, John, I can't work
here anymore. The office politics are crazy and I don't think you
manage your team well and I've lost 11 pounds since I started working
here. So with that, I won't be continuing as an employee." My boss
wasn't shocked, he accepted and I went my own way…into the jungle
of motherhood and even more crazy closed-in stay-at-home mom
activities…staying in the house and kitchen throughout the whole
summer. I felt the need to make fresh from scratch meals for breakfast,
lunch and dinner. I never left the kitchen…and my daughter and
husband and even the dog were happy as clams. Yes, I made our first
dog, Juvat (whom I was not originally fond of until we got a better
understanding of each other), homemade biscuits and, yes, he liked
them. It was 2009 and in addition to his full time job, Jerome was
working a part-time job that he hated at the pet store. Our goal was to
help us financially while I was a stay-at-home, sometimes working
mom. I was pregnant again and decided to start my life coaching
practice with a few clients here and there. I started that practice before I
knew I was expecting again. I know—off track. So back to the pet
store…Kayla and I decided to visit dad at his side job so we walked
into the pet store and the pet adoptions were on… I fell for a homeless
cat. (*To audience*) I know, always picking up the ones who don't have
nothing. (*To JEROME*) Can we get him, please? He was the only cat
who gave me attention when Kayla and I went in.

JEROME

There is no way.

TRENA
(*With puppy dog eyes*)

Please?

JEROME

If he is there after a week, then, maybe.

TRENA

Yes, it is true, Jerome's a softy. With a dog, a cat, two-year-old Kayla and a newborn on the way, I felt like my house and head were full. I know, it is not like I had ten kids already at home…yet my life was totally different from what I planned it to be…Actor. Sales Associate. Program Director. Career Counselor. Consultant. Life Coach. African American Liaison. Actor. Life Coach. Mother. Writer. Whew!

(*Lights shift*)

SCENE 6

TRENA

I would joke with my husband-to-be regularly, "You know when we get married, you are going to have to take care of me. I want a big house and a nice car." Little did I know I would end up doing the care-taking while traveling all over the world with my family far, far away from what drove me to excitement. It is June 2010 and I just received a grant from the Minnesota State Arts Board and I was back at it! I was over the moon with landing the grant. My husband on the other hand, was feeling unfulfilled in his career and desperately needed a change. One day, Jerome called me on the phone while at my newly acquired part-time job, a job I had only been on for a few weeks.

(*Cell phone rings*)

JEROME

Hon, are you able to talk?

TRENA
(*Looking around to see if anyone is watching*)
Yes. What's up?

(*TRENA gets up from the cubicle and walks outside.*)

JEROME

Hon, I got a call from D.C.

TRENA

Really!

(*Looking around while walking to her car. TRENA gets in.*)

JEROME

The State Department gave me an offer!

TRENA
(*Screech*)
Oh My Goodness! CONGRATULATIONS! When do they want you to start?
JEROME

In July.

TRENA

July? Hon, it is June. I just took this job. This July?

JEROME

This July.

(*Record scratch*)

TRENA
(*Silence*)
Okay. This means that I will have to quit my job, and I just started.

JEROME

Hon, I know, but this will be a wonderful opportunity for us. Don't you want to travel and see the world!?

TRENA

I wanted to say, "Not really," and "What about the grant I just got?" (*To audience*) Ya'll, I kept trying to get back to it—to perform another play. But what came out instead was…"Yes. I'll have to tell my supervisors right away." Really? Did I really say yes? Again? Like I wanted to be trekking around the world living in paid-for housing and meeting fabulous new people…But, to my dismay, the preparing began…really first my mental process about it and then seven days before the moving truck came…I started to organize our things…did I get it all organized? No, the house was a mess, but I tried. As I was moving on, I needed to not forget the biggest part of me. I called together a group of friends who I formally called my "wisdom circle" to help me process what type of work I could do while on this new venture, yes, journey…experience, if you will. I spread the table. I laid it out. I had drinks and food. I organized a chart and had handouts for what I thought would be a deep engaging conversation. (*Passing out information sheets about her career and work life.*) Thank you all for being here. As you know, I am great at program and leadership development, pulling communities together, marketing and event planning. I love, absolutely love, performing and helping others to achieve their goals. So with this new life that you all know (*Smiles tentatively*) Jerome and I are embarking on, what do you think I should do as my career while Jerome is having us travel all over the world?

(*TRENA shares a nervous smile.*)

WISE PERSON #1

Trena, honey, you will not be able to be as busy as you are now. You will need to stay focused on your family and keeping house.

WISE PERSON #2

Yeah, Trena, you have a husband, who is now a diplomat, to think about and little kids. Those kids are going to need you to be present.

TRENA

(*To self*)

Who started all this? Me? What was I thinking?

WISE PERSON #3

Yes, they are going to need your energy and calmness with this transition. You are going to have to help everyone transition.

TRENA

What my very wise and well-meaning wisdom circle failed to tell me was that I would be the one needing some care during my transition. What did I look like? The great Trena who takes care of all others? Forgetting self-love, self-preservation and self-expression?

WISE PERSON #4

Trena, you will be the one keeping everything together for the family.

TRENA

There goes another one....what did they know? News alert! A person can't continue to run around...do for others, forgetting about what they built and stay sane…..I now know 'cause I tried it and it didn't work. Before we left our home, family and friends, I had a real tough time with the transition. (*Crying, to JEROME*) But, I got a great life and career here. I just got a grant to create and perform a show here, and now you want me to let it all go?

JEROME

Trena, this is what I want to do with my career and I am asking you to accompany me, not half time, but full time. I really want you there.

TRENA

Well, we can get a divorce if I can't do my own creative work! (*Aside*) Creative work, yes, I am finally remembering what was so important to me.

JEROME

Okay. If that is what you want, but that is not what I want.

TRENA

(*Deflated*)

Okay, divorce is not what I want either. If you want me to go though, you have to ask me to…you can't just assume I'm going to follow you wherever you choose.

JEROME

(*Inhales deeply*)

Okay. Will you please accompany me on this journey as a U.S. Foreign Service Officer for the State Department?

TRENA

I don't know. Maybe.

(*JEROME throws his hands up.*)

TRENA (*cont.*)

Okay. I will. But now we have to renew our vows.

JEROME

(*Just about exasperated*)

Okay, whatever it takes.

TRENA

We packed, sold household items, and had four days of movers packing all of our belongings. We spent time saying goodbye to friends and loved ones, prepared our two-year-old, Kayla and nine-month-old, Annaleece for the journey. With plane tickets in hand, we drove to my parents' house in Crystal to say our last goodbyes. Being melodramatic, I made Jerome hold to renewing our vows in front of our family. Yes, we did, I needed something to hold on to. I know, I am being dramatic.

JEROME

I, Jerome Fields, take you Trena Bolden Fields, to be my wife, before God…

TRENA

(*To audience*)

Yes! He really believes in God!

JEROME

…who brought us together through his grace. I will cherish our union and love you more each day than I did the day before….

TRENA
(*To audience*)
I think he had to really think about the last part of that sentence.

JEROME

…I will trust you and respect you, laugh with you and cry with you…

TRENA
(*To audience*)

I am crying now.

JEROME

… care for you in sickness and in health, loving you faithfully through times of fortune

TRENA
(*To audience*)
My fortune is the arts, doing my creative work!

JEROME

and adversity…triumph and disaster…

TRENA
(*To audience*)
Why is he wishing bad things on me?

JEROME

…regardless of what obstacles we may face together, I give you my hand, my heart, and my love, from this day forward as long as we both shall live. Okay. Let's go!

TRENA
(*To audience*)

Off we went to D.C.

(*Lights shift*)

SCENE 7
(*Apartment in D.C. The whole family is sleeping. It is 5 a.m.*)

CAT
MEEERRROW. MEEERROW. MEEERROW.

TRENA
(*Whispers loudly*)
Shut up. Shut up! It is too early.

CAT
MEEERRROW. MEEERROW. MEEERROW.

TRENA
(*Gets up and grabs a spray bottle of water. Opens the door and sprays the cat who takes off running.*)
Sounding like a wounded child. He needs to stop before I put *him* in time out.

CAT
(*Back at the door*)
MEEERRROW. MEEERROW. MEEERROW.

TRENA
That's it!

(*TRENA opens the door, and sprays the cat with a water-bottle. Baby ANNALEECE starts fussing. TRENA goes and gets the baby and rocks her back to sleep. Agitated.*)

TRENA (*cont.*)
Who needs rest when they are running after a nine-month-old and an almost three-year-old and are supposed to be caring for the husband…Not me. Not me.

(*Baby falls back to sleep. TRENA puts her down and goes back to bed. The alarm clock goes off.*)

JEROME
Good morning, Honey!

TRENA
(*Grumpily*)

Hey.

JEROME

You know, we have the etiquette training today. We did call a baby-sitter, right?

TRENA

Yes. (*Aside*) We?

JEROME

Okay, well, you better get going so we can get out of here on time.

TRENA

Off we went on another journey for being a U.S. Foreign Service Officer. Etiquette class! You know, I just about lasted all of a few seconds…with seven different butter knives and 15 different drinking glasses for wine, champagne, water, scotch and whatever else. I decided at that very moment that we would be the "new" diplomats…the ones that were extremely informal. The following week, we invited a few colleagues and their families, who either had been posted in Hermosillo, Mexico or were on their way there, to our home... I invited everyone to bring a dish, and we ate it potluck style. No fancy smancy glasses or butter knives. The paper cups and plates worked just fine. Yes, even for these Diplomats including Jerome's new boss. (*To guests*) Y'all can get your own plate. (*To audience*) Ten months in D.C. and we were on our way to Mexico, but not before I got a chance to perform in the inaugural season at Arena Stage's renovated theatre. What? How did this happen? Jerome, God bless him, saw my sadness and searched for auditions for me in D.C. I went on two and was booked for the roll of the stenographer in the premier of the stage adaptation of *A Time to Kill*. The reviews were good for me, painting me as an actor who was definitely believable in the role…like they could see me on *Law & Order*…No skills lost…I would have loved to keep performing there, but as interruptions go…

(*Lights shift*)

SCENE 8
(*In our home in Mexico*)

TRENA

Mexico brought along another set of challenges for me: language barriers, I spoke no Spanish before moving there, fear, isolation, anger, and more fear. In the beginning, I was frustrated 95% of the time. (*To two-year-old ANNALEECE and four-year-old KAYLA*) Annaleece!...Kayla! Did you draw on the wall?

KAYLA

No!

ANNALEECE

No!

TRENA

Well, who did it?

KAYLA
(*Shrugs her shoulders*)

Anybody!

TRENA

You mean nobody, but we are the only ones in the house so somebody did it.

ANNALEECE
(*Copies KAYLA*)

It was anybody!

TRENA

I grab them both by their arms and angrily walk them to time out. Situations like this happened every time the girls did something that a child would do experimenting and trying out things I felt were wrong. I would blow up and put them in time out. Yes, I know I was back to being unhappy. Just a few months earlier, I was in the kitchen doing dishes. (*Looking around*) Annaleece, where are you?

(*Sound of a child laughing while splashing in water*)

TRENA (*cont.*)

I get up the stairs and around the corner and into her room, past her closet and into their bathroom. My two-year-old is naked using my stainless steel water bottle as a toy in the toilet...pushing her pooh in different directions, making different shapes and molds using my favorite eco-friendly water bottle. (*To ANNALEECE*) What in the world are you doing? No! No! No!

(*ANNALEECE begins to cry*)

TRENA (*cont.*)

Get over here! That is nasty! Yucky. You do not play with your pooh! You do not play in the toilet...especially with my water bottle! I had just filled my water bottle with fresh clean water. I can't believe this. You cannot play with pooh. That is nasty.

(*Pause*)

(*TRENA looks ashamed and begins to cry.*)

TRENA (*cont.*)
(*Murmuring to self*)
I can't believe I lost my temper.

(*TRENA cleans up ANNALEECE as tears stream down her face. TRENA looks towards ANNALEECE. Becomes stoic. Dresses her. Picks her up. Sits and rocks. TRENA continues to rock in silence.*)

TRENA (*cont.*)
Jerome came home from work wondering what was going on. I had nothing to say.

(*JEROME walks in and gently takes the baby from her. TRENA walks into their shared bedroom. More tears. SHE cries.*)

TRENA (*cont.)*
Later that evening, I finally fess up to my husband. (*To JEROME*) I yelled at her and told her pooh was yucky. She had my water bottle and was pushing her pooh around with it in the toilet. (*Silence. JEROME listens.*) Honey, I hope Annaleece will be okay. I did not mean to make her feel so bad.

JEROME

She will be okay. She is resilient.

TRENA

I really want to be doing what I feel passionate about. And there are times I feel trapped in this house with the bars on the windows and doors, having to clean the house from top to bottom. I want to be…(*Sniffling*)…acting or working on some project and not cleaning up poop or cleaning all day every day. I mean, look at you. I see you getting up and out to do what you love. I also see how you care for yourself every day. You put yourself first…I mean you make sure to shower and dress before facing the world…and I am still in my robe, hair uncombed at 12 noon and running ragged after the kids.

JEROME

Okay, hon, begin to do the work. Bring in the income and we can hire a part-time nanny while you take care of yourself and work on your projects.

TRENA

Did it really happen that way? No. Like I could focus… (*Pause*) Let me tell you what really went down. I spent the better time of our life in Mexico searching Facebook and lamenting on what to do next. When I noticed there were writing and theatre programs I could apply to, weighing my options to be with family while studying, I decided to apply for low residency MFA in Creating Writing programs. My justification: I can get a terminal degree for being creative and teach at the college level if I choose. My thought: I could stay with my family and move from city to city or country to country while in the program. I remember my personal purpose statement I'd been working on: "to create original works that transforms people's lives."

(*Lights shift*)

SCENE 9
(*We hear kids playing and jiggling a door knob.*)

KAYLA
(*Face pressed against the door*)
Mommy, did you lock the door? I can hear you!

TRENA
(*Sliding down the closed door*)
You know, there are times in life when we need to take a break. We just made it to the hotel after a four-hour drive from Mexico to Arizona…Yes, me and the girls, by myself. Why? Because, Jerome had to work a little longer than planned. We travelled from Mexico to Arizona to pick up the grandparents, with a seven seater mini-van, two large car seats, kids' paraphernalia, and our luggage. At that moment, I needed to go to the bathroom...really I needed a break from the crying, clinging and sisterly annoyance.

(*TRENA remembers the car ride.*)

KAYLA
Mommy, Annaleece hit me!

ANNALEECE
Mommy, Kaya hit me!

(*TRENA goes back to telling the story.*)

TRENA
Where was my husband? Still traveling from the border to Tucson. So I ran away to the bathroom...for a moment. I mean, we were in a small hotel room with a double bed—I really wasn't hiding.

TRENA
(*Quickly opens and closes and locks the door*)
They are rolling on the floor.

KAYLA
(*Giggling and banging on the door*)
Mommy, did you lock the door? I can hear you!

TRENA

Giving attention to kids is overrated. I needed to be attentive to my own needs for a change. (*Taking the moment and gathering self*) That drive and border crossing was rough.

(*We hear the girls squealing, laughing, and then sounds of pushing at each other*)

TRENA (*cont.*)
(*To self*)

Okay, let's try this again. (*Puts on a smile and walks out the bathroom door*) You want Mommy to read you a bedtime story?

KAYLA
(*Prances around*)

Yes!

ANNALEECE
(*Jumps up and down*)

Yay!

TRENA

Thank God it was time for bed. Getting the parents and getting back to Mexico was so much easier. The grandparents were there and there were three of them! Our week with the grandparents was everything I dreamed it to be! Live-in babysitters and, yes, house cleaners. Oh, no that is not all I think about my parents. Really, I love my parents, but they also need to serve some new purpose, right? Right! And we had the best time…Jerome and I did, by getting out and seeing more of the city at night while the grandparents managed the house. I tell you, generational living is not as bad as some Americans think. After the grandparents left, I felt reenergized for what I could do. My excitement lasted a little while until I heard…

JEROME

Hon, what do you think about me doing an unaccompanied tour?

(*Record scratch*)

(*Pause*)

TRENA

What - do - you - mean?

JEROME

Well, we could make more money which would help us.

TRENA

Okay…thinking about it…thinking about it…thinking about it. Uh, how about no! Not ever!

JEROME

I have to do an unaccompanied tour at some point in my career. It is now or later.

(*Pause*)

TRENA
(*To audience*)

You know I had to pray…"God if you want this to happen, let him get an opportunity to be at a great post. God I know you got this! I will be closer to family and I will be able to focus on my career. Yes, Lord. I know you got this." Then I had to talk it out with Jerome…I want you around for the girls. They are growing up and they are at the age where they know who you are…They will definitely need both of us in their teenage years… (*To audience*) You know we tossed this thought around for days, even weeks…And then I said to Jerome…so I guess if it is only a year, we can do it now. (*Takes a deep breath*) Okay, go for it. I will move home to Minnesota. (*To audience*) Who was I kidding…I had no clue how to be a mom *with* my husband…what was I going to do with two strong-willed kids by myself for a year?! Yes, I would have family nearby, but honestly they had their own lives to lead and were not always available for my every call; and what about my career? But, what I needed to focus on was the looming four-day packing of our household items.

(*TRENA is surrounded by a lot of stuff.*)

TRENA (*cont.*)

I felt the need to shut my eyes and hope that when I opened them, I would awaken from this dream of always sorting, packing and moving…just to do it all over again. I didn't know what to do with all this stuff. I took the essentials and left the rest to be donated or tossed…(*Tossing items in two different bins*) donated or tossed. Giving it all away…thinking about tossing my career in the trash…so we…

TRENA (*cont.*)
moved from Mexico, to D.C. for three months and then, I, back to
Minnesota to live solo with two young'uns.

(*Lights shift*)

SCENE 10

KAYLA
Now, go and get started on your homework.

TRENA
Back in Minnesota without Jerome, I tried to keep the girls and myself busy while rolling with it. No, I did not have those live-in baby-sitters and house cleaners anymore. I'd just begun to rebuild my coaching business and was working on writing for a film project. I was also going to make sure that I made it through this mom alone situation.

(TRENA is sitting at her desk writing. Six-year-old KAYLA enters.)

KAYLA
Mommy, when is Daddy going to be home?

TRENA
Honey, um, in a little while. (*To audience*) It was more like in a few months.

KAYLA
Where did you say he was at? Pakistan.

TRENA
Yes, honey, Pakistan. He will be home, but it will be a little while, okay.

KAYLA
Okay.

TRENA
Now, go and get started on your homework.

KAYLA
Awww. I don't want to!

TRENA
Yeah, but I want you to be an intelligent child so, please start your homework.

KAYLA
I don't want to!

TRENA
I know, but I need you to do your homework.

KAYLA

No!

TRENA

If you don't sit down and do your homework, you will have to go to bed early. (*KAYLA falls to the floor, rolling around in protest and crying.*) GET UP, GET UP right now and go to your room.

KAYLA

That's not fair!

(*KAYLA storms off to her room and shuts the door.*)

TRENA

A lot was not fair. Especially for me wanting so much and working so hard with little appreciation! Where are her grandmothers…aunties…grandfathers…anybody? One auntie showed up for me on July 4th when my youngest, who was now four, shared her thoughts on what was not fair.

ANNALEECE

Mommy, I want a corndog.

TRENA

Honey, we just had barbecue at home before coming here. (*To audience*) My whole family, excluding my out-of-country working husband, decided to go and watch the fireworks at the river that summer. We had never been to the river on the Fourth of July…so it is understandable that she'd want everything she saw…but, I say, "I am not buying any corndogs."

ANNALEECE

But, I am hungry. I want mini-donuts too. And that light-up toy over there.

TRENA

Honey, I am not buying any food. We just had a big meal. We are here to watch the fireworks. Let's do that and enjoy being with family.

ANNALEECE

I want a corndog!

TRENA

Honey, we are not getting a corndog. You can ask your aunt to buy you a light-up toy if you want to, but that is it. (*To audience*) When I can, I love using my sister as a pawn to get the kids to stop begging me for things…I have learned the art of using this as one of my go-to tools whenever we are out with my family. (*ANNALEECE runs off-stage*) Thank God! Off she goes. Right after the fireworks, it started again.

(*ANNALEECE returns*)

ANNALEECE

Mommy, I want mini-donuts.

TRENA

Honey, since the fireworks are done, the venders are not selling any food.

ANNALEECE

But, I want it, and you're being mean!

TRENA
(*To audience*)

Did I tell you this child was four years old? And then I started to act like one of those "new age" moms. (*Very sweetly to ANNALEECE*) Annaleece, I am not getting donuts right now. (*To audience*) It was almost 10:30 p.m., way past the kids' bedtime as we walked to the car. My daughter stared at me, her stare of "I'm blowing you up with my eyes" look. Yes! The laser death stare.

(*Does the stare*)

ANNALEECE

I hate you!

TRENA
(*To audience*)

Yeah… did I mention she was four? I am like "this is starting already." It kind of scared me, though. What child does that?

(*TRENA does the stare*)

TRENA (*cont.*)

Boy those were the days I wished my husband was the one receiving the laser death stare so I could claim the good parent role...yeah, no, it was just me this year. Back at home, I put the girls to bed. I was exhausted and it was also time for me to get some sleep for a change, but at 1 a.m. our normal night routine started...

KAYLA

Mommy, I can't sleep. There is a monster under Annaleece's bed.

ANNALEECE

Yes, Mommy, can we sleep with you?

TRENA
(*To audience*)

Thinking about arms across my head and feet in my back, I told the girls to go back to bed.

ANNALEECE

But, Mommy, I am scared.

KAYLA

Yeah, we want to sleep with you.

TRENA

No, girls, you are going to sleep in your own beds tonight. (*To audience*) I get up and begin to walk them to their rooms. Tears begin.

ANNALEECE

No, no, no Mommy. I want to sleep with you!

KAYLA

Yeah, we want to sleep with you.

TRENA
(*To audience*)

I hadn't had a full night's sleep since my mother-in-law's visit for Easter. Something scary started to gurgle up inside me. (*To the girls in a scary voice*) GO TO BED! DO YOU WANT ME TO TURN INTO VAMPIRE MOMMY?

(*KAYLA and ANNALEECE both laugh*)

KAYLA

Mommy, you are not vampire mommy.

TRENA

I guess, I turned into a laughable zombie, but it got the kids to bed and I got a better night's rest. The best thing, Dad was due home the next month! But oh, wait a minute, we had to begin packing for the next move…I said to myself, "I've been here before. I can do this." So we sorted, packed and headed to South Africa.

(Lights shift)

SCENE 11

(*Sound of a car crash*)

TRENA

We had just relocated and been in the country for about a month when the unprepared for happened. I was T-boned by another car while traveling through an intersection. I remember, I got hit. The car spun out to the right and my heart rattled inside my chest cavity, bouncing from the left to the right side of my rib cage. I screamed and yelled, a sound of disbelief. The shock of it all settled in. I got out the car and kept walking towards the Embassy until; someone stopped me and sat me down. "Ma'am, you are not okay." I remember hearing a man say.

(*Sirens*)

TRENA (*cont.*)

Minor whiplash. The doctor said. Said that I had to rest and take it easy for a while, but I would have a full recovery. Whoa! Wait a minute. S-L-O-W down. Did he say rest? We just got to South Africa and before the move, I spent almost every waking hour packing, shipping, driving our mini-van from Minnesota to D.C., and preparing to be in this country…and we just got our stuff shipped to us. Boy, did we have a lot to unpack. I tried to have the capacity to do all the things I needed to do while "resting." Read, write, and respond to people. I tried. But I couldn't keep my eyes open. I slept for hours at a time. Based on the amount of time I slept, it was obvious I needed to heal from something. I needed to heal from it all. My system had been shocked more times than I could count. Not doing what I loved consistently, moving to D.C., then to Mexico, back to D.C., back to Minnesota, back to D.C., then South Africa and still reeling from the grant that I left behind. The honest truth, I was in shock, still trying to get over the whiplash, the suffering from many hard stops and dealing with the emotion of packing up my life in service. My life really shifted when I became the "travelling spouse." Yeah some of you know the frequently asked question… "So *you* are the traveling spouse?" Was that who I would become? The car accident was a wake-up call to stop, slow down, and process it all. I floated through months of fuzziness until I realized how fuzzy I had been. I lost relationships and struggled with losing and letting go of my own career, my sense of identity. I was angry at my husband for "bringing" this on me. (*To JEROME*) Jerome, I really feel the need to do more of the work I want to do and I can't do that moving all over the place. I feel trapped at times and I want to blame you.

JEROME

It is so cool that we are able to experience the world. Remember it is your attitude that really shapes your experiences in life.

TRENA

Really? I am trying to talk to you here and express my feelings. I need you to listen.

JEROME

I'm sorry, hon. How can I support you? I am here to listen.

TRENA

I feel the need to build something and it is really frustrating when I am barely able to start something 'cause we move so much. I am tired of these interruptions.

JEROME

It's alright hon, life happens sometimes and interruptions take place, but you got to take time to recover and learn how to roll with it...You ready for bed?

(*JEROME and TRENA head to bed.*)

TRENA

What do you really want to do with your life?

JEROME

What I am doing.

TRENA

The Foreign Service.

JEROME

Yes, you know, become a career ambassador.

TRENA

I think that is great honey, but I am not sure how many big moves like this I can take. I really want to be in a place where I can build community and do creative work.

JEROME

Hon, you are very creative and you can create community wherever we are. Like the community you built when we were in Mexico...I know you remember going out with the ladies every month and when it was time for us to move, you had like 12 despedidas just for you... and the community you created with the other moms in D.C. and just like the community you are creating here in South Africa with the moms at gymnastics. Hon, I love you. I want you to be happy. I want you to fulfill your purpose.

TRENA

Yeah. Good night. (*Murmurs*) Love you. (*To audience*) I think I take a lot of things for love. Honestly, the truth stings sometimes, yet with the right acceptance, the antibiotic ointment begins to heal the wounds. I finally accepted where I was in life (my first application) and who were the most important in my life (my second application) and began to develop ways I could be creative and still be with my family. You see, I decided to take responsibility for my life, what I created and what I wanted to create. I then decided that I didn't have to fulfill my purpose using one medium. I could choose to use many or few and I had the power to make that decision and take action (the working ointment that is continuing to help me). Not too long ago, during preparation for my last writing course in my MFA program, I decided to apply for the Minnesota Fringe and spend two months finishing my work back in Minnesota. My husband messaged me...

JEROME

Hon, I love you! I want you to be happy. Go and fulfill your purpose.

TRENA

I made sure to keep a copy of that message so I can show it to him if he ever needs a reminder...or if I ever begin to think I need to get permission from someone else to be me. Struggling with "raising" a family according to what society and my culture had taught me, I have come through it to a place of knowing. Yes, I am still learning and traveling the globe following my husband around the world. The difference today is I am also working and doing what I feel moves me. I am writing and acting tonight, which is the best thing this creative performer could ask for. I even find time to rest and take showers. Isn't it more about how we navigate this life? I know. Cliché. My two beautiful daughters and loving husband are in town traveling with me and coming to support my career, too. The most fun part is that I get to

TRENA (*cont.*)

wake up to sharing my identity, my dreams with my little loves. Yes, today, I call them my little loves.

CAT

MEOW.

TRENA

Oh, don't you start! (*Laughs*) Okay, I love you, too, Oliver. Kisses. Mwah!

DOG

Woof!

TRENA
(*Hanging in there*)

Yes. (*Hard exhale*) You, too, Truman. Kis…how about a hug?

JEROME

What about me?

TRENA
(*Slyly*)

I guess, I love you.

(*JEROME and TRENA embrace*)

KAYLA

Mom, Mom, Mom!

TRENA

Yes, love.

KAYLA

Guess what?

TRENA

What?

KAYLA

You are the best mom ever!

TRENA

Aw, thank you! Kisses. Mwah! I love you Kayla.

KAYLA

I love you too Mom! Can I get a cupcake?

TRENA

You can get a cupcake after dinner. (*To ANNALEECE*) I love you, Annaleece.

ANNALEECE
(*Smiling bashfully*)

Me too!

TRENA

Thank you, baby! Kisses. Mwah! (*To audience*) Holding my daughters, enjoying family moments or hearing my daughters' long, drawn-out stories, shows me that I do have an even greater purpose to fulfill. My future, their future depends on it. The deep love my girls receive from me and the courage they see in me following my dreams, will help them learn to live satisfying lives and do more good in the world. The honest truth is, I want to be here and I want to have my life interrupted regularly by them.

Lights fade to black.

ABOUT THE AUTHOR

Trena Bolden Fields is a writer, actor, international speaker, and life coach. She published her first book, *For Love* in 2013 and has written two plays *Daring to Think, Move and Speak* (2011) and *My Life Interrupted, Not Once, but Forever* (2015).

Bolden Fields received her undergraduate degree in theatre arts and mass communication from Augsburg College and a master's degree in educational psychology, counseling and student personnel psychology from the University of Minnesota. She went on to study life coaching and received her life coaching certification from Adler Graduate School and then an MFA in creative writing from Augsburg College.

www.ingramcontent.com/pod-product-compliance
Lightning Source LLC
Chambersburg PA
CBHW071745020426
42331CB00008B/2186